OUT FROM THE HEART

JAMES ALLEN

Published by True Sign Publishing House
Address: SY. No. 21/2 & 21/3, Sonnenahalli,
Krishnarajapural, Bengaluru,
Karnataka - 560049 India
E-mail: truesignbooks@gmail.com
Website: www.truesign.in

Out from the Heart
Author: James Allen

ISBN: 978-93-5462-516-9

First Edition: 2021

Contents

Foreword

Confucius said , “The perfecting of one’s self is the fundamental base of all progress and all moral development”; a maxim as profound and comprehensive as it is simple , practical and uninvolved , for there is no surer way to knowledge , nor no better way to help the world than by perfecting one’s self. Nor is there any nobler work or higher science than that of self-perfection. He who studies how to become faultless , who strives to be pure hearted , who aims at the possession of a calm, wise, and seeing mind , engages in the most sublime task that man can undertake , and the results of which are perceptible in a well-ordered , blessed and beautiful life.

CHAPTER-1

The Heart and The Life

AS THE HEART, SO IS THE LIFE. The within IS ceaselessly becoming the without. Nothing remains unrevealed. That which is hidden is but for a time; it ripens and comes forth at last. Seed, tree, blossom, and fruit are the fourfold order of the universe. From the state of a man's heart proceed the conditions of his life. His thoughts blossom into deeds; and his deeds bear the fruitage of character and destiny.

Life is ever unfolding from within, and revealing itself to the light, and thoughts engendered in the heart at last reveal themselves in words, actions, and things accomplished.

As the fountain from the hidden spring, so flows forth a man's life from the secret recesses of his heart. All that he is and does is generated there. All that he will be and do will take its rise there.

Sorrow and happiness, suffering and enjoyment, fear and hope, hatred and love, ignorance and enlightenment, are nowhere but in the heart. They are solely mental conditions.

Man is the keeper of his heart; the watcher of his mind; the solitary guard of his citadel of life. As such, he can be diligent or negligent. He can keep his heart more and more carefully. He can more strenuously watch and purify his mind; and he can guard against the thinking of unrighteous thoughts—this is the way of enlightenment and bliss.

On the other hand, he can live loosely and carelessly, neglecting the supreme task of rightfully ordering his life—this is the way of self-delusion and suffering.

Let a man realize that life in its totality proceeds from the mind, and lo, the way of blessedness is opened up to him! For he will then discover that he possesses the power to rule his mind, and to fashion it in accordance with his Ideal. So will he elect to strongly and steadfastly walk those pathways of thought and action which are altogether excellent. To him, life will become beautiful and sacred; and sooner or later, he will put to flight all evil, confusion, and suffering. For it is impossible for a man to fall short of liberation, enlightenment, and peace, who guards with unwearying diligence the gateway of his heart.

CHAPTER-2

The Nature and Power of Mind

MIND IS THE ARBITER of life. It is the creator and shaper of conditions, and the recipient of its own results. It contains within itself both the power to create illusion and to perceive reality. Mind is the infallible weaver of destiny. Thought is the thread, good and evil deeds are the "warp and woof" or foundation, and the web, woven upon the loom of life, is character. Mind clothes itself in garments of its own making.

Man, as a mental being, possesses all the powers of mind, and is furnished with unlimited choice. He learns by experience, and he can accelerate or retard his experience. He is not arbitrarily bound at any point, but he has bound himself at many points, and having bound himself he can, when he chooses, liberate himself.

He can become bestial or pure, ignorant or noble, foolish or wise, just as he chooses. He can, by reoccurring practice, form habits, and he can, by renewed effort, break them off. He can surround himself with illusions until Truth is completely lost, and he can destroy each of those illusions until Truth is entirely recovered. His possibilities are endless; his freedom is complete.

It is the nature of the mind to create its own conditions, and to choose the states in which it shall dwell. It also has the power to alter any condition, to abandon any state. This it is continually doing as it gathers knowledge of state after state by repeated choice and exhaustive experience.

Inward processes of thought make up the sum of character and life. Man can modify and alter these processes by bringing will and effort to bear upon them. The bonds of habit, impotence, and sin are self-made, and can only be destroyed by one's self. They exist nowhere but in one's mind, and although they are directly related to outward things, they have no real existence in those things.

The outer is molded and animated by the inner, and never the inner by the outer. Temptation does not arise in the outer object, but in the lust of the mind for that object. Nor do sorrow and suffering belong by nature to the external things and happenings of life, but in an undisciplined attitude of mind toward those things and happenings.

The mind that is disciplined by Purity and fortified by Wisdom avoids all those lusts and desires which are inseparately bound up with affliction, and so arrives at enlightenment and peace.

To condemn others as evil, and to curse at outside conditions as the source of evil, increases and does not lessen, the world's suffering and unrest. The outer is but the shadow and effect of the inner, and when the heart is pure all outward things are pure.

All growth and life is from within outward; all decay and death is from without inward. This is the universal law. All evolution proceeds from within. All adjustment must take place within. He who ceases to strive against others, and employs his powers in the transformation, regeneration, and development of his own mind, conserves his energies and preserves himself. And as he succeeds in harmonizing his own mind, he leads others by consideration and charity into a like blessed state.

The way of enlightenment and peace is not gained by assuming authority and guidance over other minds, but by exercising a lawful authority over one's own mind, and by guiding one's self in pathways of steadfast and lofty virtue.

A man's life proceeds from his heart and his mind. He has compounded that mind by his own thoughts and deeds. It is within his power to refashion that mind by his choice of thought. In this manner he can transform his life. Let us see how this is to be done.

CHAPTER-3

Formation of Habit

EVERY ESTABLISHED mental condition is an acquired habit, and it has become such by continuous repetition of thought. Despondency and cheerfulness, anger and calmness, covetousness and generosity—indeed, all states of mind—are habits built up by choice, until they have become automatic. A thought constantly repeated at last becomes a fixed habit of the mind, and from such habits proceeds one's life.

It is in the nature of the mind to acquire knowledge by the repetition of its experiences. A thought which is very difficult, at first, to hold and dwell upon, at last becomes, by constantly being held in the mind, a natural and habitual practice.

A boy, when commencing to learn a trade, cannot even handle his tools right, much less use them correctly, but after long repetition and practice, he plies them with perfect ease and consummate skill. Likewise, a state of mind, at first apparently incapable of realization, is, by perseverance and practice, at last acquired and built into the character as a natural and spontaneous condition.

In this power of the mind to form and reform its habits, its conditions, is contained the basis of a man's salvation.

It is the open door to perfect liberty by the mastery of self. For as a man has the power to form harmful habits, so he equally has the same power to create habits that are essentially good. And here we come to a point which needs some clarifying, and which calls for deep and earnest thought on the part of my reader.

It is commonly said to be easier to do wrong than right, to sin than to be holy. Such a condition has come to be regarded, almost universally, as a self-evident truth.

No less a teacher than the Buddha has said: "Bad deeds, and deeds hurtful to ourselves, are easy to do; what is beneficial and good, that is very difficult to do."

And with regards to humanity generally, this is true, but it is only true as a passing experience, a fleeting factor in human evolution. It is not a fixed condition of things. It is not the nature of an eternal truth. It is easier for men to do wrong than right, because of the prevalence of ignorance, because the true nature of things, and the essence and meaning of life, are not understood.

When a child is learning to write, it is extremely easy to hold the pen wrongly, and to form his letters incorrectly, but it is painfully difficult to hold the pen and to write properly. This is because of the child's ignorance of the art of writing, which can only be dispelled by persistent effort and practice, until, at last, it becomes natural and easy to hold the pen correctly, and difficult, as well as altogether unnecessary, to do the wrong thing.

It is the same in the vital things of mind and life. To think and do rightly requires much practice and renewed effort. But the time comes at last when it becomes habitual and easy to think and do rightly, and difficult, as it is then seen to be altogether unnecessary, to do that which is wrong.

Just as an artisan becomes, by practice, accomplished in his craft, so you can become, by practice, accomplished in goodness. It is entirely a matter of forming new habits of thought. And he to whom right thoughts have become easy and natural, and wrong thoughts and acts difficult to do, has attained to the highest virtue, to pure spiritual knowledge.

It is easy and natural for men to sin because they have formed by incessant repetition, harmful and unenlightened habits of thought. It is very difficult for the thief to refrain from stealing when the opportunity occurs, because he has lived so long in covetous and greedy thoughts.

But such difficulty does not exist for the honest man who has lived so long with upright and honest thoughts. He has thereby become so enlightened as to the wrong, folly, and fruitlessness of theft, that even the remotest idea of stealing does not enter his mind. The sin of theft is a very extreme one, and I have introduced it in order to more clearly illustrate the force and formation of habit. But all sins and virtues are formed in the same way.

Anger and impatience are natural and easy to thousands of people, because they are constantly repeating angry and impatient thoughts and acts. And with each repetition the habit is more firmly established and more deeply rooted.

Calmness and patience can become habitual in the same way—by first grasping through effort, a calm and patient thought, and then continuously thinking it, and living in it, until "use becomes second nature," and anger and impatience pass away forever. It is in this manner that every wrong thought may be expelled from the mind; that every untrue act may be destroyed; that every sin may be overcome.

CHAPTER-4
Doing and Knowing

LET A MAN REALIZE that his life, in its totality, proceeds from his mind. Let him realize that the mind is a combination of habits which he can, by patient effort, modify to any extent, and over which he can thus gain complete ascendancy, mastery, and control. At once, he will have obtained possession of the key which shall open the door to his complete emancipation.

But freedom from the ills of life (which are the ills of one's mind) is a matter of steady growth from within, and not a sudden acquisition from without. Hourly and daily must the mind be trained to think stainless thoughts, and adapt right and dispassionate attitudes under those circumstances in which it is prone to fall into wrong and passion. Like the patient sculptor upon his marble, the aspirant to the Right Life must gradually work upon the crude material of his mind until he has wrought out of it the Ideal of his holiest dreams.

In working toward such supreme accomplishment, it is necessary to begin at the lowest and easiest steps, and proceed by natural, progressive stages to the higher and more difficult. This law of growth, progress, evolution, and unfoldment, by gradual and ever ascending stages, is absolute in every department of life, and in every human accomplishment. Where it is ignored, total failure will result.

In acquiring education, in learning a trade, or in pursuing a business, this law is fully recognized and minutely obeyed by all. But in acquiring Virtue, in learning Truth, and in pursuing the right conduct and knowledge of life, it is unrecognized and disobeyed by nearly all. Hence Virtue, Truth, and the Perfect Life remain unpracticed, unacquired, and unknown.

It is a common error to suppose that the Higher Life is a matter of reading, and the adoption of theological or metaphysical hypotheses, and that Spiritual Principles can be understood by this method. The Higher Life is higher living in thought, word, and deed, and the knowledge of those Spiritual Principles which are imminent in man and in the universe can only be acquired after long discipline in the pursuit and practice of Virtue.

The lesser must be thoroughly grasped and understood before the greater can be known. Practice always precedes real knowledge.

The schoolmaster never attempts to teach his pupils the abstract principles of mathematics at the start. He knows that such a method of teaching would be in vain, and learning impossible. He first places before them a simple sum, and, having explained it, leaves them to do it. When, after repeated failures and ever renewed effort, they have succeeded in doing it correctly, a more difficult task is set before them, and then another and another. It is not until the pupils have, through many years of diligent application, mastered all the lessons in arithmetic, that he attempts to unfold to them the underlying mathematical principles.

In learning a trade, say that of a mechanic, a boy is not at first taught the principles of mechanics, but a simple tool is put in his hand and he is told how rightly to use it. He is then left to do it by effort and practice. As he succeeds in plying his tools correctly, more and more difficult tasks are set before him, until after several years of successful practice, he is prepared to study and grasp the principles of mechanics.

In a properly governed household, the child is first taught to be obedient, and to conduct himself properly under all circumstances. The child is not even told why he must do this, but is commanded to do it. Only after he has far succeeded in doing what is right and proper, is he told why he should do it. No father would attempt to teach his child the principles of ethics before exacting from him the practice of family duty and social virtue.

Thus practice ever precedes knowledge even in the ordinary things of the world, and in spiritual things, in the living of the Higher Life, this law is rigid in its demands.

Virtue can only be known by doing, and the knowledge of Truth can only be arrived at by perfecting oneself in the practice of Virtue. To be complete in the practice and acquisition of Virtue is to be complete in the knowledge of Truth.

Truth can only be arrived at by daily and hourly doing the lessons of Virtue, beginning with the simplest, and passing on to the more difficult. A child patiently and obediently learns his lessons at school by constantly practicing, ever exerting himself until all failures and difficulties are surmounted. Likewise does the child of Truth, undaunted by failure, and made stronger by difficulties, apply himself to rightdoing in thought and action. As he succeeds in acquiring Virtue, his mind unfolds itself in the knowledge of Truth, and it is a knowledge in which he can securely rest.

CHAPTER-5

First Steps in The Higher Life

SEEING THAT THE PATH OF VIRTUE is the Path of Knowledge, and that before the all-embracing Principles of Truth can be comprehended, perfection in the more lowly steps must be acquired, how, then, shall a disciple of Truth begin?

How shall one who aspires to the righting of his mind and the purification of his heart—that heart which is the fountain and repository of all the issues of life—learn the lessons of Virtue? How does he thus build himself up in the strength of knowledge, destroying ignorance and the ills of life? What are the first lessons, the first steps? How are they learned? How are they practiced? How are they mastered and understood?

The first lessons consist in overcoming those wrong mental conditions which are most easily eradicated, and which are the common barriers to spiritual progress, as well as in practicing the simple domestic and social virtues. The reader will be better aided if I group and classify the first ten steps in three lessons as follows: Vices of the Body to be Overcome and Eradicated

(First Lesson: Discipline of the Body)

1st step: Idleness, Laziness or Indolence

2nd step: Self-Indulgence or Gluttony

(Second Lesson: Discipline of Speech)

3rd step: Slander

4th step: Gossip and Idle Conversation

5th step: Abusive and Unkind Speech

6th step: Frivolity or Irreverent Speech

7th step: Critical, Captious or Fault-finding Speech

(Third Lesson: Discipline of Tendencies)

8th step: Unselfish Performance of Duty

9th step: Unswerving Rectitude or Moral Integrity

10th step: Unlimited Forgiveness

The two vices of the body, and the five of the tongue, are so called because they are manifested in the body and tongue. Also, by so definitely classifying them, the mind of the reader will be better helped. But it must be clearly understood that these vices arise primarily in the mind, and are wrong conditions of the heart worked out in the body and the tongue.

The existence of such chaotic conditions is an indication that the mind is altogether unenlightened as to the real meaning and purpose of life, and their eradication is the beginning of a virtuous, steadfast, and enlightened life.

But how shall these vices be overcome and eradicated? By first, and at once, checking and controlling their outward manifestations and by suppressing the wrong act. This will stimulate the mind to watchfulness and reflection until, by repeated practice, it will come to perceive and understand the dark, wrong, and erroneous conditions of mind, out of which such acts spring. It will then abandon them entirely.

It will be seen that the first step in the discipline of the mind is the overcoming of indolence or laziness. This is the easiest step, and until it is perfectly accomplished, the other steps cannot be taken. The clinging to indolence constitutes a complete barrier to the Path of Truth. Indolence consists in giving the body more ease and sleep than it requires, in procrastinating, and in shirking and neglecting those things which should receive immediate attention.

This condition of laziness must be overcome by rousing up the body at an early hour, giving it just the amount of sleep it requires for complete recuperation, and by doing promptly and vigorously, every task, every duty, no matter how small, as it comes along.

On no account should food or drink be taken in bed. And to lie in bed after one has awakened, indulging in ease and reverie, is a habit fatal to promptness and resolution of character, and purity of mind. Nor should one attempt to do his thinking at such a time. Strong, pure, and true thinking is impossible under such circumstances. A man should go to bed to sleep, not to think. He should get up to think and work, not to sleep.

The next step is the overcoming of self-indulgence or gluttony. The glutton is he who eats for animal gratification only, without considering the true end and object of eating. He eats more than his body requires, and is greedy after sweet things and rich dishes.

Such undisciplined desire can only be overcome by reducing the quantity of food eaten, and the number of meals per day, and by resorting to a simple and uninvolved diet. Regular hours should be set apart for meals, and eating at other times should be rigidly avoided. Suppers should be abolished, as they are altogether unnecessary, and promote heavy sleep and cloudiness of mind.

The pursuit of such a method of discipline will rapidly bring the once ungoverned appetite under control, and as the sensual sin of self-indulgence is taken out of the mind, the right selection of foods will be instinctively and infallibly adapted to the purified mental condition.

It should be well borne in mind that a change of heart is the needful thing, and that any change of diet which does not promote this end is futile. When one eats for enjoyment, he is gluttonous. The heart must be purified of sensual craving and gustatory lust.

When the body is well controlled and firmly guided; when that which is to be done is done vigorously; when no task or duty is delayed; when early rising has become a delight; when frugality, simplicity, temperance, and abstinence are firmly established; when one is contented with the food which is put before him, no matter how scanty and plain, and the craving for gustatory pleasure is at an end—then the first two steps in the Higher Life are accomplished. Then is the first great lesson in Truth learned. Thus is established in the heart the foundation of a poised, self-governed, virtuous life.

The next lesson is the lesson of Virtuous Speech, in which there are five orderly steps. The first of these is overcoming the habit of slanderous speech. Slander consists of inventing or repeating unkind and evil reports about others, in exposing and magnifying the faults of others, or of absent friends, and in introducing unworthy insinuations. The elements of thoughtlessness, cruelty, insincerity, and untruthfulness enter into every slanderous act.

He who aims at the living of the right life will commence to check the cruel word of slander before it has gone forth from his lips. He will then check and eliminate the insincere thought which gave rise to it.

He will watch that he does not vilify or defame anyone. He will refrain from disparaging, defaming, and condemning the absent friend, whose face he has so recently smiled into or kissed, or whose hand he has shaken. He will not say of another that which he dare not say to his face. Thus, coming at last to think sacredly of the character and reputation of others, he will destroy those wrong conditions of mind which give rise to slander.

The next step is the overcoming of gossip and idle conversation. Idle speech consists in talking about the private affairs of others, in talking merely to pass away the time, and in engaging in aimless and irrelevant conversation. Such an ungoverned condition of speech is the outcome of an ill-regulated mind.

The man of virtue will bridle his tongue, and thus learn how rightly to govern the mind. He will not let his tongue run idly and foolishly, but will make his speech strong and pure, and will either talk with a purpose or remain silent.

Abusive and unkind speech is the next vice to be overcome. The man who abuses and accuses others has himself wandered far from the Right Way. To hurl hard words and names at others is to sink deeply into folly. When a man is inclined to abuse, curse, and condemn others, let him restrain his tongue and look within himself. The virtuous man refrains from all abusive language and quarreling. He employs only words that are useful, necessary, pure, and true.

The sixth step is the overcoming of levity, or irreverent speech. Light and frivolous talking; the repeating of crude jokes; the telling of vulgar stories, having no other purpose than to raise an empty laugh; offensive familiarity, and the employment of contemptuous and disrespectful words when speaking to or of others, and particularly of one's elders and those who rank as one's teachers, guardians or superiors—all of this will he put away by the lover of Virtue and Truth.

Upon the altar of irreverence absent friends and companions are immolated for the passing excitement of a momentary laugh, and all the sanctity of life is sacrificed to the zest for ridicule. When respect towards others and the giving of reverence where reverence is due are abandoned, Virtue is abandoned. When modesty, significance, and dignity are eliminated from speech and behavior, Truth is lost. Yea, even its entrance gate is hidden away and forgotten.

Irreverence is degrading even in the young, but when it accompanies grey hairs, and appears in the demeanor of the preacher—this is indeed a piteous spectacle. And when this can be imitated and followed after, then are the blind leading the blind, then have elders, preachers, and people lost their way.

The virtuous will be of earnest and reverent speech. He will think and speak of the absent as he thinks and speaks of the dead—tenderly and sacredly. He will put away thoughtlessness, and watch that he does not sacrifice his dignity to gratify a passing impulse to frivolity and superficiality. His humor will be pure and innocent, his voice will be subdued and musical, and his soul will be filled with grace and sweetness as he succeeds in conducting himself as becomes a man of Truth.

The last step in the second lesson is the overcoming of criticism, or fault-finding speech. This vice of the tongue consists in magnifying and harping on small or apparent faults, in foolish quibbling and hair-splitting, and in pursuing vain arguments based upon groundless suppositions, beliefs, and opinions.

Life is short and real, and sin, sorrow and pain are not remedied by carping and contention. The man who is ever on the watch to catch at the words of others in order to contradict and dispute them, has yet to reach the higher way of holiness, the truer life of self-surrender. The man who is ever on the alert to check his own words in order to soften and purify them will find the higher way and the truer life. He will conserve his energies, maintain his composure of mind, and preserve within himself the spirit of Truth.

When the tongue is well controlled and wisely subdued; when selfish impulses and unworthy thoughts no longer rush to the tongue demanding utterance; when the speech has become harmless, pure, gentle, gracious, and purposeful, and no word is uttered but in sincerity and honesty—then are the five steps to virtuous speech accomplished, then is the second great lesson in Truth learned and mastered.

And now some will ask, "But why all this discipline of the body and restraint of the tongue? Surely the Higher Life can be realized and known without such strenuous labor, such incessant effort and watchfulness?" No, it cannot. In the spiritual as the material, nothing is done without labor, and the higher cannot be known until the lower is fulfilled.

Can a man make a table before he has learned how to handle a tool and drive a nail? And can a man fashion his mind in accordance with Truth before he has overcome the slavery of his body?

As the intricate subtleties of language cannot be understood and wielded before the alphabet and the simplest words are mastered, neither can the deep subtleties of the mind be understood and purified before the ABC of right conduct is perfectly acquired.

As for the labor involved—does not the youth joyfully and patiently submit himself to a seven-years' apprenticeship in order to master a craft? And does he not, day by day, carefully and faithfully carry out every detail of his master's instructions, looking forward to the time when, perfected through obedience and practice, he shall be himself a master?

Where is the man who sincerely aims at excellence in music, painting, literature, or in any trade, business, or profession who is not willing to give his whole life to the acquirement of that particular perfection? Shall labor, then, be considered where the very highest excellence is concerned—the excellence of Truth?

He who says, "The Path which you have pointed out is too difficult; I must have Truth without labor, salvation without effort," that man will not find his way out of the confusions and sufferings of selfhood. He will not find the calm, well-fortified mind and the wisely ordered life. His love is for ease and enjoyment, and not for Truth.

He who, deep in his heart, adores Truth, and aspires to know it, will consider no labor too great to be undertaken, but will adopt it joyfully and pursue it patiently. By perseverance in practice he will come to the knowledge of Truth.

The necessity for this preliminary discipline of the body and tongue will be more clearly perceived when it is fully understood that all these wrong outward conditions are merely the expressions of wrong conditions of the heart. An indolent body means an indolent mind; an ill-regulated tongue reveals an ill-regulated mind, and the process of remedying the manifested condition is really a method of rectifying the inward state.

Moreover, the overcoming of these conditions is only a small part of what is really involved in the process. The ceasing from evil leads to, and is inseparably connected with, the practice of good. While a man is overcoming laziness and self-indulgence, he is really cultivating and developing the virtues of abstinence, temperance, punctuality, and self-denial. He is acquiring the strength, energy, and resolve which are indispensable to the successful accomplishment of the higher tasks. While he is overcoming the vices of speech, he is developing the virtues of truthfulness, sincerity, reverence, kindliness, and self-control, and is gaining that mental steadiness and fixedness of purpose, without which the more remote subtleties of the mind cannot be regulated, and the higher stages of conduct and enlightenment cannot be reached.

Also, as he has to do right, his knowledge deepens, and his insight is intensified. Just as a child's heart is glad when a school task is mastered, so with each victory achieved, the man of virtue experiences a bliss which the seeker after pleasure and excitement can never know.

And now we come to the third lesson in the Higher Life, which consists of practicing and mastering, in one's daily life, three great fundamental Virtues:

1. Unselfish Performance of Duty
2. Unswerving Rectitude (Moral Integrity)
3. Unlimited Forgiveness

Having prepared the mind by overcoming the more surface and chaotic conditions mentioned in the first two lessons, the striver after Virtue and Truth is now ready to enter upon greater and more difficult tasks, and to control and purify the deeper motives of the heart.

Without the right performance of duty, the higher virtues cannot be known, and Truth cannot be apprehended. Duty is generally regarded as an irksome labor, a compulsory something which must be toiled through, or be in some way avoided. This way of regarding duty proceeds from a selfish condition of mind, and a wrong understanding of life. All duty should be regarded as sacred, and it s faithful and unselfish performance one of the leading rules of conduct. All personal and selfish considerations should be extracted and cast away from the doing of one's duty, and when this is done, duty ceases to be irksome, and becomes joyful. Duty is only irksome to him who craves some selfish enjoyment or benefit for himself. Let the man who is chafing under the irksomeness of his duty look to himself, and he will find that his wearisomeness proceeds, not from the duty itself, but from his selfish desire to escape it.

He who neglects duty, be it great or small, or of a public or private nature, neglects Virtue. He who in his heart rebels against duty, rebels against Virtue. When Duty becomes a thing of love, and when every particular duty is done accurately, faithfully, and dispassionately, there is much subtle selfishness removed from the heart, and a great step is taken towards the heights of Truth. The virtuous man concentrates his mind on the perfect doing of his own duty, and does not interfere with the duty of another.

The ninth step is the practice of Unswerving Rectitude or Moral Integrity. This Virtue must be firmly established in the mind, and so enter into every detail of a man's life. All dishonesty, deception, trickery, and misrepresentation must be forever put away, and the heart purged of every vestige of insincerity and deception. The least digression from the path of rectitude or righteousness is a deviation from Virtue.

There must be no extravagance and exaggeration of speech, but the simple truth should be stated. Engaging in deception, no matter how apparently insignificant, for boastful pride, or with the hope of personal advantage, is a state of delusion which one should make efforts to dispel. It is demanded of the man of Virtue that he shall not only practice the most rigid honesty in thought, word, and deed, but that he shall be exact in his statements, omitting and adding nothing to the actual truth.

In thus shaping his mind to the principle of Rectitude or moral integrity, he will gradually come to deal with people and things in a just and impartial spirit, considering equity before himself, and viewing all things with freedom from personal bias, passion, and prejudice. When the Virtue of Rectitude is fully practiced and comprehended, so that all temptation to untruthfulness and insincerity has ceased, then is the heart made purer and nobler. Then is character strengthened, and knowledge enlarged, and life takes on a new meaning and a new power. Thus is the ninth step accomplished.

The tenth step is the practice of Unlimited Forgiveness. This consists in overcoming the sense of injury which springs from vanity, selfishness and pride; and in exercising disinterested charity and large-heartedness towards all. Spite, retaliation, and revenge are so utterly ignoble, so base, and so small and foolish, as to be altogether unworthy of being noticed or harbored. No one who fosters such conditions in his heart can lift himself above folly and suffering, and guide his life aright. Only by casting them away, and ceasing to be moved by them, can a man's eyes be opened to the true way of life. Only by developing a forgiving and charitable spirit can he hope to approach and perceive the strength and beauty of a well-ordered life.

In the heart of the strongly virtuous man, no feeling of personal injury can arise. He has put away all retaliation, and has no enemies. If other men should regard themselves as his enemies, he will regard them kindly, understanding their ignorance, and making full allowance for it.

When this state of heart is arrived at, then the tenth step in the discipline of one's selfseeking inclinations is accomplished. Then the third great lesson in Virtue and Knowledge is learned and mastered.

Having thus laid down the first ten steps and three lessons in right-doing and rightknowing, I leave those of my readers who are prepared for them to learn and master them in their everyday life.

There is, of course, a still higher discipline of the body, a more far-reaching discipline of the tongue, and greater and more all-embracing virtues to acquire and understand before the highest state of bliss and knowledge can be grasped. But it is not my purpose to deal with them here. I have expounded only the first and easiest lessons on the Higher Path, and by the time these are thoroughly mastered, the reader will have become so purified, strengthened, and enlightened, that he will not be left in the dark as to his future progress.

Those of my readers who have completed these three lessons will already have perceived, beyond and above, the high altitudes of Truth, and the narrow and precipitous track which leads to them, and will choose whether they shall proceed.

The straight Path which I have laid down can be pursued by all with greater profit to themselves and to the world. And even those who do not aspire to the attainment of Truth, will develop greater intellectual and moral strength, finer judgment, and deeper peace of mind by perfecting themselves in this Path. Nor will their material prosperity suffer by this change of heart; nay, it will be rendered truer, purer, and more enduring. For if there is one who is capable of succeeding and fitted to achieve, it is the man who has abandoned the petty weaknesses and everyday vices of his kind, who is strong enough to rule his body and mind, and who pursues with fixed resolve the path of unswerving integrity and sterling virtue.

CHAPTER-6

Mental Conditions and Their Effects

WITHOUT GOING into the details of the greater steps and lessons in the right life (a task outside the scope of this small work) a few hints concerning those mental conditions from which life in its totality springs seem in order. These hints will prove helpful to those who are ready and willing to penetrate further into the inner realm of heart and mind where Love, Wisdom, and Peace await the rapidly progressing student of life.

All sin is ignorance. It is a condition of darkness and undevelopment. The wrongthinker and the wrong-doer is in the same position in the school of life as the ignorant pupil in the school of learning. He has yet to learn how to think and act correctly, that is, in accordance with Law. The pupil in learning is not happy so long as he does his lessons wrongly. Likewise, unhappiness cannot be escaped while sin remains unconquered.

Life is a series of lessons. Some are diligent in learning them, and they become pure, wise, and altogether happy. Others are negligent, and do not apply themselves. They remain impure, foolish, and unhappy.

Every form of unhappiness springs from a wrong condition of mind. Happiness is inherent in right conditions of mind. Happiness is mental harmony, unhappiness is mental inharmony. While a man lives in wrong conditions of mind, he will live a wrong life, and will suffer continually.

Suffering is rooted in error. Bliss is inherent in enlightenment. There is salvation for man only in the destruction of his own ignorance, error, and self-delusion. Where there are wrong conditions of mind there is bondage and unrest. Where there are right conditions of mind there is freedom and peace.

Here are some of the leading wrong mental conditions and their disastrous effects upon one's life:

1. *Hatred*—which leads to injury, violence, disaster, and suffering.
2. *Lust*—which leads to confusion of intellect, remorse, shame, and wretchedness.
3. *Covetousness*—which leads to fear, unrest, unhappiness, and loss.
4. *Pride*—which leads to disappointment, humiliation, and lack of self-knowledge.
5. *Vanity*—which leads to distress and mortification of spirit.
6. *Condemnation*—which leads to persecution and hatred from others.
7. *Ill-will*—which leads to failures and troubles.
8. *Self-indulgence*—which leads to misery, loss of judgment, grossness, disease, and neglect.

9. *Anger*—which leads to the loss of power and influence.
10. *Desire or Self-slavery*—which leads to grief, folly, sorrow, uncertainty, and loneliness.

The above wrong conditions of mind are merely negations. They are states of darkness and deprivation and not of positive power. Evil is not a power; it is ignorance and misuse of good. The hater is he who has failed to do the lesson of Love correctly, and he suffers in consequence. When he succeeds in doing it rightly, the hatred will have disappeared, and he will see and understand the darkness and impotence of hatred. This is so with every wrong condition.

The following are some of the more important right mental conditions and their beneficial effects upon one's life:

1. *Love*—which leads to gentle conditions, bliss, and blessedness.
2. *Purity*—which leads to intellectual clearness, joy, invincible confidence.
3. *Selflessness*—which leads to courage, satisfaction, happiness, and abundance.
4. *Humility*—which leads to calmness, restfulness, knowledge of Truth.
5. *Gentleness*—which leads to emotional equilibrium, contentment under all circumstances.
6. *Compassion*—which leads to protection, love, and reverence from others.

7. *Goodwill*—which leads to gladness, success.
8. *Self-control*—which leads to peace of mind, true judgment, refinement, health, and honor.
9. *Patience*—which leads to mental power, far-reaching influence.
10. *Self-conquest*—which leads to enlightenment, wisdom, insight, and profound peace.

The above right conditions of mind are states of positive power, light, joyful possession, and knowledge. The good man knows. He has learned to do his lessons correctly, and thereby understands the exact proportions which make up the sum of life. He is enlightened, and he knows good and evil. He is supremely happy, doing only that which is divinely right.

The man who is involved in the wrong conditions of mind, does not know. He is ignorant of good and evil, of himself, of the inward causes which make his life. He is unhappy, and believes other people are entirely the cause of his unhappiness. He works blindly, and lives in darkness, seeing no central purpose in existence, and no orderly and lawful sequence in the course of things.

He who aspires to the attainment of the Higher Life in its completion—who would perceive with unveiled vision the true order of things and the meaning of life—let him abandon all the wrong conditions of the heart, and persevere unceasingly in the practice of good. If he suffers, or doubts, or is unhappy, let him search within until he finds the cause, and having found it, let him cast it away. Let him so guard and purify his heart that every day less of evil and more of good shall issue therefrom. So he will daily become stronger, nobler, and wiser. So will his blessedness increase, and the Light of Truth, growing ever brighter and brighter within him, will dispel all gloom, and illuminate his Pathway.

CHAPTER-7

Exhortation

DISCIPLES OF TRUTH, lovers of Virtue, seekers of Wisdom; you, also, who are sorrow stricken, knowing the emptiness of the self-life, and who aspire to the life that is supremely beautiful, and serenely joyful—take now yourselves in hand, enter the Door of Discipline, and know the Better Life.

Put away self-delusion. Behold yourself as you are, and see the Path of Virtue as it is. There is no lazy way to Truth. He who would stand upon the mountain's summit must strenuously climb, and must rest only to gather strength. But if the climbing is less glorious than the cloudless summit, it is still glorious. Discipline in itself is beautiful, and the end result of discipline is sweet.

Rise early and meditate. Begin each day with a conquered body, and a mind fortified against error and weakness. Temptation will never be overcome by unprepared fighting. The mind must be armed and arrayed in the silent hour. It must be trained to perceive, to know, to understand. Sin and temptation disappear when right understanding is developed.

Right understanding is reached through unabated discipline. Truth cannot be reached but through discipline.

Patience will increase by effort and practice, and patience will make discipline beautiful.

Discipline is irksome to the impatient man and the lover of self, so he avoids it, and continues to live loosely and confusedly.

Discipline is not irksome to the lover of Truth, and he will find the infinite patience which can wait, work, and overcome. Just as the joy of the gardener who sees his or her flowers develop day by day, so is the joy of the man of discipline who sees the divine flowers of Purity, Wisdom, Compassion, and Love, grow within his heart.

The loose-liver cannot escape sorrow and pain. The undisciplined mind falls, weak and helpless, before the fierce onslaught of passion.

Array well your mind, then, lover of Truth. Be watchful, thoughtful, and resolute. Your salvation is at hand; your readiness and effort are all that are needed. If you fail ten times, do not be disheartened. If you should fail a hundred times, rise up and pursue your way. If you should fail a thousand times, do not despair. When the right Path is entered, success is sure if the Path is not utterly abandoned.

First strife, and then victory. First labor, and then rest. First weakness, and then strength. In the beginning the lower life, and the glare and confusion of battle, and at the end the Life Beautiful, the Silence, and the Peace.

All common things, each day's events, That with the hour begin and end; Our pleasures and our discontents Are rounds by which we may ascend. We have not wings, we cannot soar; But we have feet to scale and climb.

Longfellow

* * *

www.ingramcontent.com/pod-product-compliance
Lightning Source LLC
LaVergne TN
LVHW101955220826
846093LV00006B/234